The Farmer's Daughter Block

A Classic For Today's Quilts

Building Blocks Series 1 — Book 2

Special thanks to the following
for the beautiful fabrics used
in the quilts in this book:

Marcus Fabrics

Northcott

RJR Fabrics

Robert Kaufman Fabrics

All quilt designs by Sandy Boobar and
Sue Harvey of Pine Tree Country Quilts,
www.pinetreecountryquilts.com.

Published by

All American Crafts, Inc.
7 Waterloo Road
Stanhope, NJ 07874
www.allamericancrafts.com

Publisher | **Jerry Cohen**

Chief Executive Officer | **Darren Cohen**

Product Development
Director | **Brett Cohen**

Editor | **Sue Harvey**

Proofreader | **Natalie Rhinesmith**

Art Director | **Kelly Albertson**

Illustrations | **Kathleen Geary, Roni Palmisano
& Chrissy Scholz**

Product Development
Manager | **Pamela Mostek**

Vice President/Quilting Advertising
& Marketing | **Carol Newman**

Printed in China
ISBN: 978-1-936708-01-7
UPC: 793573035240

www.allamericancrafts.com

Contents

Table of Contents

Welcome

Welcome to the Building Blocks
series of quilting books.

Whether you're making your first or your one hundred
and first quilt, the eight books in this series will be an
invaluable addition to your quilting library. Besides fea-
turing the instructions to make a different traditional
and timeless block in each book, we've also included
charts to give you all the quick information you need to
change the block size for your own project.

Each book features complete instructions for three
different quilts using the featured block with variations
in size, color, and style—all designed to inspire you to
use these timeless blocks for quilts with today's look.

The Finishing Basics section in each book gives you the
tips and techniques you'll need to border, quilt, and bind
the quilts in this book (or any quilt you may choose to
make). If you're an experienced quilter, these books will
be an excellent addition to your reference library. When
you want to enlarge or reduce a block, the numbers are
already there for you! No math required!

The blocks in the Building Blocks series of books have
stood the test of time and are still favorites with quilters
today. Although they're traditional blocks, they look very
contemporary in today's bold and beautiful fabrics. This
definitely puts them in the category of quilting
classics!

For each block, you'll find a little background about its name, origin, or era, just to add a touch of quilting trivia. The block presented in this book is Farmer's Daughter. It is believed to have originated in Ohio in the 1850s, though, according to Barbara Brackman in her book, *Encyclopedia of Pieced Quilt Patterns*, its first publication was by Clara Stone in her *Practical Needlework: Quilt Patterns* in 1906. Between 1906 and 1934, this block was published four more times with as many different names—Rolling Stone, Jack's Blocks, Corner Posts, and Flying Birds.

The traditional block was made with template-cut pieces and set-in squares in the corners. To simplify stitching, the block in this book is pieced in three rows with only squares and rectangles.

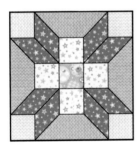
Traditional

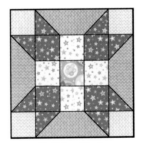
Building Block

The quilts in this book celebrate the versatility of this charming old block. From an elegant, lacy-looking bed quilt to a bouncy, colorful throw, you'll find plenty of inspiration to begin playing with color and fabrics to make this one of your favorite blocks.

Farmer's Daughter

Use these instructions to make the blocks for the quilts in this book. The materials needed for each quilt and the cutting instructions are given with the pattern for the quilt. Also included is a Build It Your Way chart with four different sizes for this block and the sizes to cut the pieces for one block. Use this information to design your own quilt or to change the size of any of the quilts in this book.

BUILDING THE BLOCK
Use a 1/4" seam allowance throughout.

1. The easiest way to piece this block for the quilts in this book, or any quilt that uses more than just a few blocks, is to begin with strip sets to make the block center. Instructions are given in the pattern for each quilt that uses this method. Refer to those instructions and then continue with step 4.

2. To piece a single block or a small number of blocks, choose the block size from the Build It Your Way chart. Cut the following pieces for each block: one A, four B, four C, eight E, and four F squares, and four D rectangles.

3. Sew an A square between two B squares. Press seams toward the A square to make an AB segment. Sew a B square between two C squares. Press seams toward the C squares to make a BC segment. Repeat to make a second BC segment. Make one AB segment and two BC segments for each block.

Make 1   Make 2

4. Sew an AB segment length-wise between two BC segments. Press seams toward the BC segments to complete one block center.

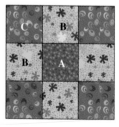

5. Mark a diagonal line on the wrong side of the E squares. Place a marked square right sides together on one end of a D rectangle. Stitch on the marked line. Trim the seam allowance to 1/4". Press the E corner to the right side.

6. Place a marked E square right sides together on the remaining end of the D rectangle. Stitch on the marked line. Trim the seam allowance to 1/4". Press E corner to the right side to complete one DE unit.

Make 4

7. Repeat steps 5 and 6 to make four DE units total.

8. Sew a DE unit to opposite sides of the block center. Press seams toward the block center. Sew an F square to each end of the remaining DE units. Press seams toward the F squares. Sew the pieced strips together to complete the block. Press seams away from the center strip.

9. Repeat to complete the number of blocks needed for the quilt that you have chosen.

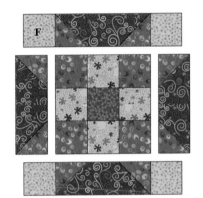

Build It Better

Having trouble matching the angled E edges to the straight edges of the block center? Mark a line 1/4" from the edge of the DE unit across the angled seams. Place the DE unit right sides together with the block center. Fold the edge of the DE unit back on the 1/4" line. The angled seams should intersect with the seams of the block center. Adjust, if necessary. Pin the pieces to hold for stitching.

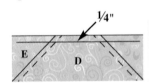

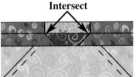

1/4" Intersect

Piece	7¹/2" Block	10" Block	12¹/2" Block	15" Block
	Build It Your Way			
A	2" x 2"	2¹/2" x 2¹/2"	3" x 3"	3¹/2" x 3¹/2"
B	2" x 2"	2¹/2" x 2¹/2"	3" x 3"	3¹/2" x 3¹/2"
C	2" x 2"	2¹/2" x 2¹/2"	3" x 3"	3¹/2" x 3¹/2"
D	2" x 5"	2¹/2" x 6¹/2"	3" x 8"	3¹/2" x 9¹/2"
E	2" x 2"	2¹/2" x 2¹/2"	3" x 3"	3¹/2" x 3¹/2"
F	2" x 2"	2¹/2" x 2¹/2"	3" x 3"	3¹/2" x 3¹/2"

Roly-Poly

Hot, hot red and cool blues and greens—what a combo! Use heat to blur the lines between blocks to make a secondary design really pop. What do you see first in this quilt? The red frames, of course!

Finished Quilt Size: 64" x 64"
Finished Block Size: $12^1/2$" x $12^1/2$"
Number of Blocks: 16
Skill Level: Beginner

MATERIALS

All yardages are based on 42"-wide fabric.

❖ $3/4$ yard of blue print
❖ $1/2$ yard of green/multi print
❖ $7/8$ yard of blue swirl print
❖ $1^1/4$ yards of red loop print
❖ $3/8$ yard of green print
❖ $3/4$ yard of yellow swirl print
❖ $2^1/8$ yards of large circle print
❖ $4^1/8$ yards of backing fabric
❖ 72" x 72" piece of batting
❖ Thread to match fabrics
❖ Rotary cutting tools
❖ Basic sewing supplies

CUTTING

Label all pieces with the letters assigned. They will be used throughout the instructions.

From the blue print, cut
- 1 A strip 3" x 42"
- 7 strips 2¹/4" x 42" for binding

From the green/multi print, cut
- 4 B strips 3" x 42"

From the blue swirl print, cut
- 4 C strips 3" x 42"
- 5 strips 3" x 42"; recut into (64) 3" E squares

From the red loop print, cut
- 7 strips 3" x 42"; recut into (32) 3" x 8" D rectangles
- 4 strips 4¹/2" x 42"; recut into (32) 4¹/2" J squares

From the green print, cut
- 3 strips 3" x 42"; recut into (32) 3" F squares

From the yellow swirl print, cut
- 1 G strip 5" x 42"
- 6 strips 2¹/2" x 42" for inner border

From the large circle print, cut
- 2 H strips 4¹/2" x 42"
- 6 strips 4¹/2" x 42"; recut into (16) 4¹/2" x 13" I rectangles
- 6 strips 5¹/2" x 42" for outer border

From the backing fabric, cut
- 2 pieces 72" long

MAKING THE FARMER'S DAUGHTER BLOCKS

Use a 1/4" seam allowance throughout unless otherwise instructed.

1. Sew a blue A strip lengthwise between two green/multi B strips. Press seams toward the A strip. Crosscut the strip set into eight 3" AB segments.

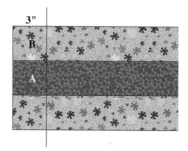

2. Sew a green/multi B strip lengthwise between two blue swirl C strips. Press seams toward the C strips. Repeat to make a second strip set. Crosscut the strip sets into (16) 3" BC segments.

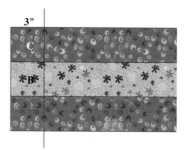

3. Refer to Building the Block on page 6, steps 4-9, to make eight 13" x 13" Farmer's Daughter blocks.

MAKING THE SNOWBALL VARIATION BLOCKS

1. Sew a yellow swirl G strip lengthwise between two large circle H strips. Press seams toward the H strips. Crosscut the strip set into eight 5" GH segments.

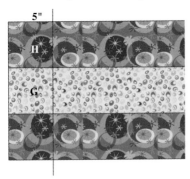

2. Mark a diagonal line on the wrong side of each red loop J square.

3. Place a marked square right sides together on each end of a large circle I rectangle. Stitch on the marked lines. Trim the seam allowances to 1/4" and press the J corners to the right side to complete an IJ unit. Repeat to make 16 IJ units total.

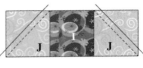

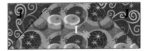

Make 16

4. Sew a GH segment lengthwise between two IJ units to complete one 13" x 13" Snowball Variation block. Repeat to make eight blocks total.

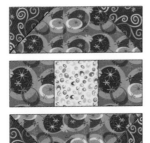

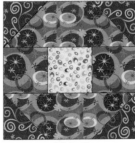

Make 8

Build It Better

Be careful of one-way fabrics when you piece the rows of this quilt! If you are using a directional fabric in place of the large circle print, you won't want to just turn every other row end for end—your print will be upside down in half the rows. Instead, make two rows that begin with a Farmer's Daughter block and two rows that begin with a Snowball Variation block. Then just alternate the rows to make the quilt center.

COMPLETING THE TOP

1. Sew two Farmer's Daughter blocks alternately together with two Snowball Variation blocks. Press seams toward the Snowball Variation blocks. Repeat to make four rows total.

2. Join the block rows to complete the 50 1/2" x 50 1/2" quilt center, turning every other row end for end. Press seams in one direction.

3. Sew the 2 1/2" x 42" yellow swirl print strips short ends together to make a long strip. Press seams in one direction. Cut into two 50 1/2" strips and two 54 1/2" strips. Sew the shorter strips to opposite sides and the longer strips to the remaining sides of the quilt center. Press seams toward the strips. *Note: Refer to Finishing Basics on page 26 for information about cutting border strips.*

4. Sew the 5 1/2" x 42" large circle print strips short ends together to make a long strip. Press seams in one direction. Cut into two 54 1/2" strips and two 64 1/2" strips. Sew the shorter strips to opposite sides and the longer strips to the remaining sides to complete the quilt top. Press seams toward the strips.

FINISHING THE QUILT

1. Remove the selvage edges from the backing pieces. Sew the pieces together down the length with a 1/2" seam allowance. Trim the sides to make a 72" x 72" backing piece. Press seam open.

2. Refer to Finishing Basics to layer, quilt, and bind your quilt.

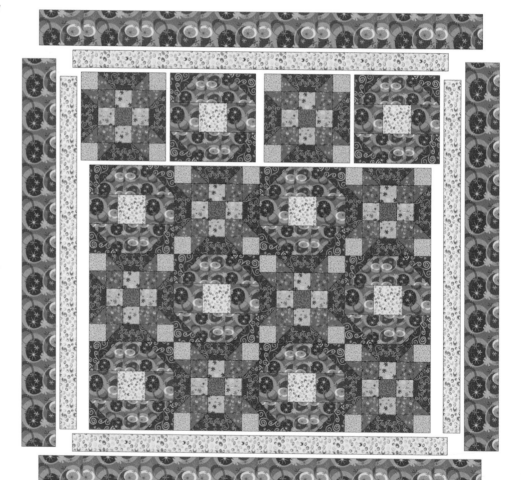

Quilt Assembly Diagram

A deep red fabric placed in the corners of the Farmer's Daughter blocks turns the frames
seen in *Roly-Poly* into background for the darker fabrics of the blocks.

Inside Out

Tired of plain borders? Just bring the inside of the quilt to the outside! Blocks in the border, whether centered on each side like this quilt, in the corners, or even going around the corners, add lots of interest. And the best part? Because the border is just an extension of the inside, there is no trying to make a completely different pieced strip fit with your quilt center.

Finished Quilt Size: 37 1/2" x 45"
Finished Block Size: 7 1/2" x 7 1/2"
Number of Blocks: 18
Skill Level: Confident Beginner/Intermediate

MATERIALS
All yardages are based on 42"-wide fabric.

❖ 7/8 yard of pink bear print
❖ 3/8 yard of white star print
❖ 3/4 yard of brown star print
❖ 2/3 yard of pink dot
❖ 1/2 yard of tan dot
❖ 1/2 yard of diagonal stripe
❖ 3 1/8 yards of backing fabric
❖ 46" x 53" piece of batting
❖ Thread to match fabrics
❖ Rotary cutting tools
❖ Basic sewing supplies

CUTTING

Label all pieces with the letters assigned. They will be used throughout the instructions.

From the pink bear print, cut
- 1 A strip 2" x 42"
- 1 strip 6¹/₂" x 42"; recut into (4) 6¹/₂" x 8" H rectangles
- 1 strip 2" x 42"; recut into (4) 2" x 6¹/₂" J strips
- 2 strips 6¹/₂" x 42"; recut into (4) 6¹/₂" x 15¹/₂" K rectangles

From the white star print, cut
- 4 B strips 2" x 42"

From the brown star print, cut
- 4 C strips 2" x 42"
- 7 strips 2" x 42"; recut into (144) 2" E squares

From the pink dot, cut
- 9 strips 2" x 42"; recut into (72) 2" x 5" D rectangles

From the tan dot, cut
- 6 strips 2" x 42"; recut into (72) 2" F squares, (4) 2" x 8" G strips, and (4) 2" x 9¹/₂" I strips

From the diagonal stripe, cut
- 5 strips 2¹/₄" x 42" for binding

From the backing fabric, cut
- 2 pieces 53" long

MAKING THE FARMER'S DAUGHTER BLOCKS

Use a ¹/₄" seam allowance throughout unless otherwise instructed.

1. Sew a pink bear A strip lengthwise between two white star B strips. Press seams toward the A strip. Crosscut the strip set into (18) 2" AB segments.

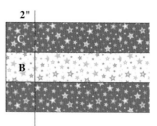

2. Stitch a white star B strip lengthwise between two brown star C strips. Press seams toward the C strips. Repeat to make a second strip set. Crosscut the strip sets into (36) 2" BC segments.

3. Refer to Building the Block on page 6, steps 4-9, to make (18) 8" x 8" Farmer's Daughter blocks. (Refer to Build It Better on page 18 for pressing tips.)

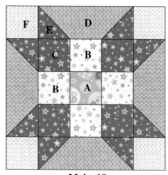

Make 18

MAKING THE BORDER UNITS

1. Sew a tan dot G strip to one 8" edge of each pink bear H rectangle to make four GH units. Press seams toward the H rectangles.

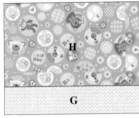

Make 4

2. Stitch a pink bear J strip to one end of each tan dot I strip to make two IJ strips and two reversed IJ strips. Press seams toward the I strips. Sew a pink bear K rectangle lengthwise to each IJ and reversed IJ strip to make two K units and two reversed K units. Press seams toward the K rectangles.

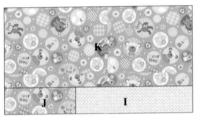

Make 2

Make 2 Reversed

COMPLETING THE TOP

1. Sew a K unit and reversed K unit to opposite sides of a Farmer's Daughter block to make the top row. Press seams toward the K units. Repeat to make the bottom row, pressing seams toward the block. (Refer to the Quilt Assembly Diagram on page 18.)

2. Join three blocks and add a GH unit to each end. Press seams toward the center block. Repeat to make row 5, pressing seams toward the GH units.

3. Join five blocks to make row 3. Press seams toward the end blocks. Repeat to make row 4, pressing seams toward the center block.

4. Sew the rows together to complete the 38" x 45½" quilt center. Press seams to one side.

FINISHING THE QUILT

1. Remove the selvage edges from the backing pieces. Sew the pieces together down the length with a ½" seam allowance. Trim the sides to make a 46" x 53" backing piece. Press seam open.

2. Refer to Finishing Basics to layer, quilt, and bind your quilt.

Build It Better

Need a throw or bed quilt? With the same number of blocks and the same arrangement, make a 50" x 60" quilt, a 62½" x 75" quilt, or a 75" x 90" quilt by using one of the larger block sizes in the Build It Your Way chart on page 7. Use the following sizes for the border units.

Piece	10" Block	12½" Block	15" Block
G	2½" x 10½"	3" x 13"	3½" x 15½"
H	8½" x 10½"	10½" x 13"	12½" x 15½"
I	2½" x 12½"	3" x 15½"	3½" x 18½"
J	2½" x 8½"	3" x 10½"	3½" x 12½"
K	8½" x 20½"	10½" x 25½"	12½" x 30½"

Quilt Assembly Diagram

Build It Better

Get your seam allowances under control to make this quilt easier to piece. When making the blocks, refer to the arrows in these block diagrams to press the seams. Make nine A blocks and nine B blocks, then alternate A and B blocks in the rows when completing the top.

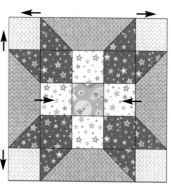

A Block
Make 9

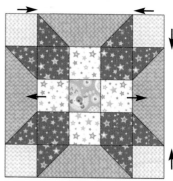

B Block
Make 9

Using a fabric with a definite top and bottom design in the border units adds another twist to cutting the pieces. Be sure to cut the H strips the height of the rectangles x 42" instead of the width x 42"—for this quilt, 8" x 42". Then be sure to sew the G strips to the right edge of two H rectangles and to the left edge of two H rectangles.

Lace Filigree

This quilt proves that one color is not boring! A variety of teal fabrics for the piecing with cream used for the background makes the X design of the blocks seem to float. The teal connects from block to block to make a lacy effect.

Finished Quilt Size: 89" x 103"
Finished Block Size: 10" x 10"
Number of Blocks: 38
Skill Level: Intermediate

MATERIALS
All yardages are based on 42"-wide fabric.

- ❖ 3/8 yard of cream filigree print
- ❖ 2 5/8 yards of green/teal floral
- ❖ 7/8 yard of light teal tonal
- ❖ 3 2/3 yards of cream tonal
- ❖ 2 1/4 yards of dark teal tonal
- ❖ 7/8 yard of light teal print
- ❖ 1 1/2 yards of cream/teal seaweed print
- ❖ 9 1/2 yards of backing fabric
- ❖ 97" x 111" piece of batting
- ❖ Thread to match fabrics
- ❖ Rotary cutting tools
- ❖ Basic sewing supplies

CUTTING

Label all pieces with the letters assigned. They will be used throughout the instructions.

From the cream filigree print, cut
- 3 A strips 2½" x 42"

From the green/teal floral, cut
- 11 B strips 2½" x 42"
- 9 strips 6½" x 42" for outer border

From the light teal tonal, cut
- 10 C strips 2½" x 42"

From the cream tonal, cut
- 10 strips 6½" x 42"; recut into (152) 2½" x 6½" D rectangles
- 3 strips 10½" x 42"; recut into (4) 10½" G squares and (4) 10½" x 20½" H rectangles
- 8 strips 3½" x 42" for inner border

From the dark teal tonal, cut
- 19 strips 2½" x 42"; recut into (304) 2½" E squares
- 10 strips 2¼" x 42" for binding

From the light teal print, cut
- 10 strips 2½" x 42"; recut into (152) 2½" F squares

From the cream/teal seaweed print, cut
- 3 strips 15³⁄₈" x 42"; recut into (5) 15³⁄₈" I squares and (2) 8" J squares, then cut each I square twice diagonally to make 20 I triangles and each J square in half diagonally to make 4 J triangles (discard 2 I triangles)

From the backing fabric, cut
- 3 pieces 111" long

MAKING THE FARMER'S DAUGHTER BLOCKS

Use a ¼" seam allowance throughout unless otherwise instructed.

1. Sew a cream filigree A strip lengthwise between two green/teal B strips. Press seams toward the B strips. Repeat to make three strip sets total. Crosscut the strip sets into (38) 2½" AB segments.

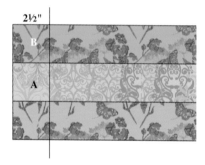

2. Stitch a green/teal B strip lengthwise between two light teal C strips. Press seams toward the B strips. Repeat to make five strip sets total. Crosscut the strip sets into (76) 2½" BC segments.

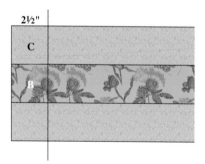

3. Refer to Building the Block on page 6, steps 4-9, to make (38) 10½" x 10½" Farmer's Daughter blocks.

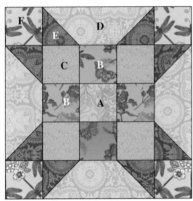

Make 38

COMPLETING THE TOP

1. Join the blocks, cream G squares and H rectangles, and cream/teal seaweed I triangles in 10 diagonal rows. Press seams in each row in one direction and in opposing directions from row to row. (Refer to the Quilt Assembly Diagram on page 24.)

2. Join the rows. Press seams in one direction. Sew a cream/teal seaweed J triangle to each angled corner to complete the 71¼" x 85¼" quilt center. Press seams toward the triangles.

3. Sew the 3½" x 42" cream tonal strips short ends together to make a long strip. Press seams in one direction. Cut into two 85¼" strips and two 77¼" strips.

Sew the longer strips to the long sides and the shorter strips to the top and bottom of the quilt center. Press seams toward the strips. *Note: Refer to Finishing Basics on page 26 for information about cutting border strips.*

4. Stitch the 6½" x 42" green/teal floral strips short ends together to make a long strip. Press seams in one direction. Cut into two 91¼" strips and two 89¼" strips. Sew the longer strips to the long sides and the shorter strips to the top and bottom to complete the quilt top. Press seams toward the strips.

FINISHING THE QUILT

1. Remove the selvage edges from the backing pieces. Sew the pieces together down the length with a ½" seam allowance. Trim the sides to make a 97" x 111" backing piece. Press seam open.

2. Refer to Finishing Basics to layer, quilt, and bind your quilt.

Build It Better

Don't let diagonal rows make you dizzy! Mark the row numbers on small pieces of paper and pin them to the top piece in each row. It's a snap to keep track of the layout and the order of the blocks in the rows.

Quilt Assembly Diagram

The lacy effect is gone in this striking version of *Lace Filigree*. The dark background and the use of several colors in the blocks create a more defined medallion look.

Finishing Basics

ADDING BORDERS

Borders are an important part of your quilt. They add another design element, and act much like a picture frame to complement and support the center.

There are two basic types of borders—butted corners and mitered corners. Butted corners are the most common. For this technique, border strips are stitched to opposite sides of the quilt center, pressed, and then strips are sewn to the remaining sides. Mitered corners are often used to continue a pattern around the corners; for example, the stripe in a fabric or a pieced border design.

Butted corners　　　　**Mitered corners**

Lengths are given for the borders in the individual quilt instructions. In most cases, fabric-width strips are joined to make a strip long enough to cut two side strips and top and bottom strips. Because of differences in piecing and pressing, your quilt center may differ slightly in size from the mathematically exact size used to determine the border lengths. Before cutting the strips for butted corners, refer to the instructions given here to measure for lengths to fit your quilt center. For mitered borders, extra length is already included in the sizes given in the instructions to make it easier to stitch the miters. It should be enough to allow for any overall size differences.

BUTTED CORNERS

1. Press the quilt center. Arrange it on a flat surface with the edges straight.

2. Fold the quilt in half lengthwise, matching edges and corners. Finger-press the center fold to make a crease. Unfold.

3. Measure along the center ceased line to determine the length of the quilt center.

 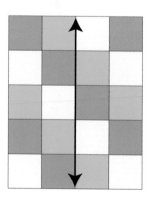

Fold in half

4. Cut two strips this length.

5. Fold the strips in half across the width and finger-press to make a crease.

6. Place a strip right sides together on one long edge of the quilt center, aligning the creased center of the strip with the center of the long edge. Pin in place at the center. Align the ends of the strips with the top and bottom edges of the quilt center. Pin in place at each end.

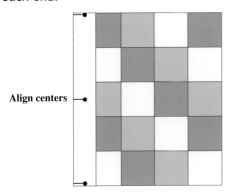

Align centers

7. Pin between the ends and center, easing any fullness, if necessary.

8. Stitch the border to the quilt center. Press.

9. Repeat on the remaining long edge.

10. Fold the quilt in half across the width and crease to mark the center. Unfold. Measure along the creased line to determine the width of the bordered quilt center.

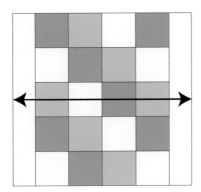

11. Cut two strips this length.

12. Repeat steps 5—9 on the top and bottom edges of the quilt center.

MITERED CORNERS

1. Prepare the border strips as directed in the individual pattern.

2. Make a mark ¹/₄" on each side of the quilt corners.

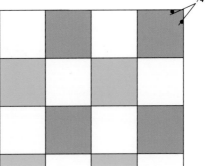

¹/₄"

3. Center the border strips on each side of the quilt top and pin in place. Stitch in place, stopping and locking stitches at the ¹/₄" mark at each corner.

4. Fold the quilt top in half diagonally with wrong sides together. Arrange two border ends right sides together.

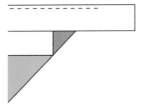

5. Mark a 45° angle line from the locked stitching on the border to the outside edge of the border.

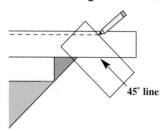

45° line

6. Stitch on the marked line, starting exactly at the locked stitch. Trim seam allowance to 1/4".

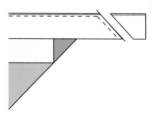

7. Press the mitered corner seam open and the seam between the border and the rest of the quilt toward the border.

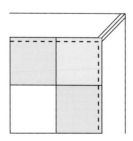

8. Repeat these steps on each corner of the quilt.

LAYERING, BASTING & QUILTING

You may choose to do your own quilting or take your projects to a machine quilter. Be sure that your backing and batting are at least 4" wider and 4" longer on each side of the quilt top. The size needed is given in the Materials list for each project.

If you would like to quilt your own project, there are many good books about hand and machine quilting. Check with your quilting friends or at your local quilt shop for recommendations. Here are the basic steps to do your own quilting:

1. Mark the quilt top with a quilting design, if desired.

2. Place the backing right side down on a flat surface. Place the batting on top. Center the quilt top right side up on top of the batting. Smooth all the layers. Thread-baste, pin, or spray-baste the layers together to hold while quilting.

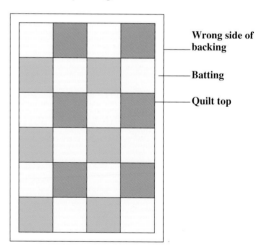

Wrong side of backing

Batting

Quilt top

3. Quilt the layers by hand or machine.
4. When quilting is finished, trim the batting and backing even with the quilted top.

BINDING

The patterns in this book include plenty of fabric to cut either 2¼" or 2½" wide strips for straight-grain, double-fold binding. In some cases, a wider binding or bias binding is needed because of a specific edge treatment; extra yardage is included when necessary.

PREPARING STRAIGHT-GRAIN, DOUBLE-FOLD BINDING

1. Cut strips as directed for the individual pattern. Remove selvage edges.

2. Place the ends of two binding strips right sides together at a right angle. Mark a line from inside corner to inside corner. Stitch on the marked line. Trim seam allowance to ¼".

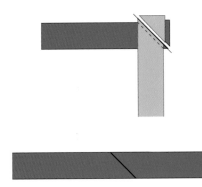

3. Repeat step 2 to join all binding strips into one long strip. Press seams to one side. Fold the strip in half lengthwise with wrong sides together and press.

PREPARING DOUBLE-FOLD BIAS BINDING

1. Cut an 18" x 42" strip from the binding fabric.

2. Place the 45˚ angle line of a rotary ruler on one edge of the strip. Trim off one corner of the strip.

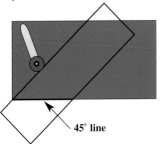

45° line

3. Cut binding strips in the width specified in the pattern from the angled end of the strip.

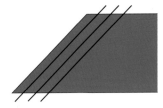

4. Each strip will be approximately 25" long. Cut strips to total the length needed for the pattern, repeating steps 1 and 2 if needed.

5. Align the ends of two strips with right sides together. Stitch ¼" from the ends.

6. Repeat to join all binding strips into one long strip. Press seams to one side.

ADDING THE BINDING

1. Leaving a 6"-8" tail and beginning several inches from a corner, align the raw edges of the binding with the edge of the quilt. Stitch along the edge with a 1/4" seam allowance, locking stitches at the beginning.

2. Stop 1/4" from the first corner and lock stitching. Remove the quilt from your machine. Turn the quilt so the next edge is to your right. Fold the binding end up and then back down so the fold is aligned with the previous edge of the quilt and the binding is aligned with the edge to your right. Starting at the edge of the quilt, stitch the binding to the next corner.

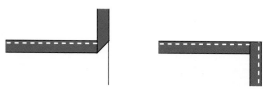

3. Repeat step 2 to attach binding to the rest of the quilt, stopping stitching 6"–8" from the starting point and locking stitches.

4. Unfold the ends of the strips. Press flat. About halfway between the stitched ends, fold the beginning strip up at a right angle. Press. Fold the ending strip down at a right angle, with the folded edge butted against the fold of the beginning end. Press.

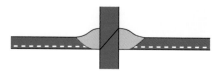

5. Trim each end 1/4" from creased fold. Place the trimmed ends right sides together. Pin to hold. Stitch 1/4" from the ends. Press the seam allowance open.

6. Refold the strip in half. Press. Arrange the strip on the edge of the quilt and stitch in place to finish the binding.

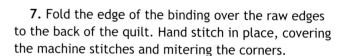

7. Fold the edge of the binding over the raw edges to the back of the quilt. Hand stitch in place, covering the machine stitches and mitering the corners.

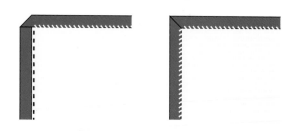

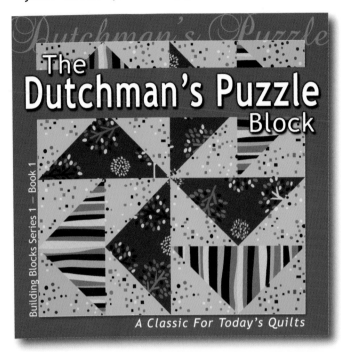

The **Dutchman's Puzzle** Block

Building Blocks Series 1 — Book 1

A Classic For Today's Quilts

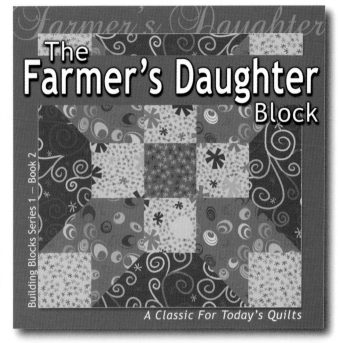

The **Farmer's Daughter** Block

Building Blocks Series 1 — Book 2

A Classic For Today's Quilts

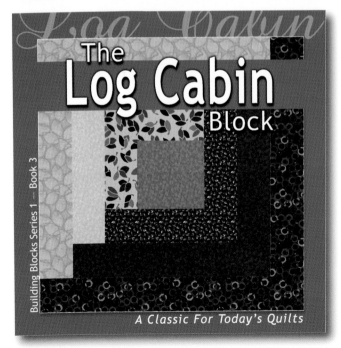

The **Log Cabin** Block

Building Blocks Series 1 — Book 3

A Classic For Today's Quilts

The **Snail's Trail** Block

Building Blocks Series 1 — Book 4

A Classic For Today's Quilts

Books 5-8 →

COLLECT THEM ALL! Look for the complete Building Blocks Series 1 Books 1–8 at your local quilt shop, favorite book store, or order ~~~~icancrafts.com.

DISCARDED

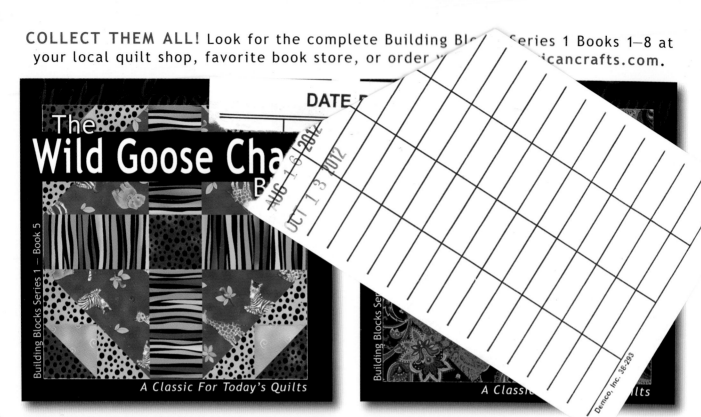

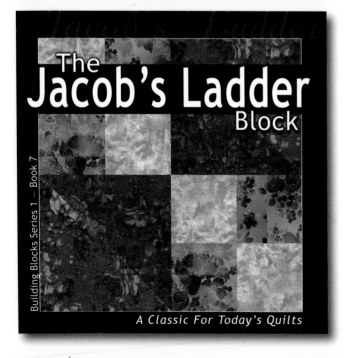

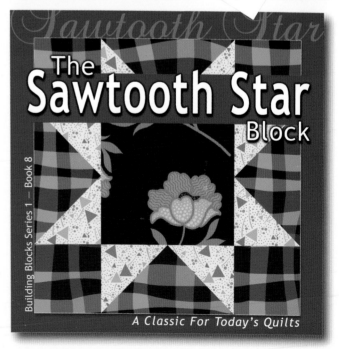